German-American Genealogical Research
Monograph Number 4

EMIGRANTS FROM SAXONY
(GRANDDUCHY OF SACHSEN-WEIMAR-EISENACH)
TO AMERICA, 1854, 1859

Clifford Neal Smith

CLEARFIELD

Reprint, 1981
Reprint, 1983
Reprint, 1986
Reprint, 1987
Reprint, 1987
Reprint, 1987   ± ∫
Reprint, 1988   qz
Reprint, 1990   qz

Reprint, 1993   u
Reprint, 1997   u

Originally published
McNeal, Arizona, 1974

Reprinted for
Clearfield Company by
Genealogical Publishing Co.
Baltimore, Maryland
2004, 2007

ISBN-13: 978-0-8063-5249-7
ISBN-10: 0-8063-5249-3

Lists of names have been taken from *Praktische Forschungshilfe: Das Suchblatt fuer Fragen der Familienforscher* and from *Archiv fuer Sippenforschung*, with permission of C. A. Starke Verlag, Limburg/Lahn, West Germany. Incidental information regarding individual emigrants has been translated from the German.

EMIGRANTS FROM SAXONY (GRANDDUCHY OF

SACHSEN-WEIMAR-EISENACH) TO AMERICA, 1854, 1859

Clifford Neal Smith

Two articles, written by Dr. Herbert Koch,[1] have appeared in
German genealogical publications regarding emigration from the Grandduchy of Sachsen-Weimar-Eisenach to America during the years 1854 and
1859.[2] Since these articles have wide implications for German-American researchers, they have been combined into one list of emigrants in
this monograph. The first of the articles, entitled "Neunzig Auswanderer aus Sachsen-Weimar 1859" [Ninety Emigrants from Saxony-Weimar,
1859] contains a list abstracted from published official notices which
were a part of the administrative procedure required for permits to
leave the country. Dr. Koch writes that he believes the list to be
almost entirely complete. Researchers should remember, however, that
some emigrants--especially young men avoiding German military service
obligations and debtors fleeing their creditors--may have emigrated
illegally and without the required official notices. Such persons
would not appear in the list hereinafter.

Dr. Koch's second article, entitled "Achthundert Auswanderer
aus Sachsen-Weimar (1854)" [Eight Hundred Emigrants from Saxony-
Weimar, 1854], makes a less sweeping claim to completeness. He points
out that his list covers only the eastern portion of the Grandduchy of
Sachsen-Weimar-Eisenach, including only the Neustadt, Jena, Weimar,
and Allstedt *Bezirke* (administrative districts), but not the western
portion of the realm (Eisenach, Gerstungen, etc.). Here, again, the

the names of emigrants have been abstracted from official notices required of legal emigrants; illegal emigrants are not included.

In general, the official notices state only that the emigrants were going to America. Some will have emigrated to Brazil, others to Canada, and probably most to the United States.

Genealogical researchers finding names of interest to them should, as a next step in proving the connection between the emigrant and his American descendants, search the passenger lists of the Hamburg police authorities (both the Direct and the Indirect series) for destinations. Microfilms of these lists may be consulted in the Manuscript Division of the Library of Congress, Washington, D.C., and in the library of the LDS Genealogical Society, Salt Lake City, Utah. Check first the microfilm for the index (alphabetische) volumes of both the Direct and Indirect series. This will give the volume and page number in the ship-list (chronologische) volumes. The ship lists give name, age, place of origin, profession, ship's name, and destination for each emigrant. Having established the emigrant's identity and American port of entry, researchers should then be able to locate the American arrival list in the National Archives, Washington, D.C.

Surnames underscored in the following list pertain to persons who emigrated in 1859, or shortly thereafter. Surnames *not* underscored pertain to persons who emigrated in 1854, or shortly thereafter. These dates are particularly important when entering either the Hamburg departure lists or the American arrival lists on file in the National Archives, Washington, D.C.

1. Dr. Koch's address in 1959 was:

> Dr. Herbert Koch,
> <u>Jena</u>,
> Prof.-Ibrahim-Strasse 35,
> DDR (German Democratic Republic)

In the first of his articles, Dr. Koch invited inquiries from interested researchers abroad and hoped that his list would be of use to German-Americans.

2. The two articles are:

Herbert Koch, "Neunzig Auswanderer aus Sachsen-Weimar 1859," *Praktische Forschungshilfe: Das Suchblatt für alle Fragen der Familienforscher* (Limburg/Lahn: C. A. Starke Verlag), 25. Jahrgang, Band 2, neue Folge, Heft 2 (May 1959), pp. 88-89.

Herbert Koch, "Achthundert Auswanderer aus Sachsen-Weimar (1854)," *Archiv für Sippenforschung* (Limburg/Lahn: C. A. Starke Verlag), 27. Jahrgang (1961), pp. 131-136.

4

Emigrant's Name	Place of Origin	Remarks
ABT, Johann Christian Heinrich	Kranichfeld	Master shoemaker; with wife Marie Therese and 1 child
ADOLARIUS, Karl	Martinroda	
ALPERSTEDT, Johann	Stotternheim	with wife and 4 children
AMERELL, Carl Bernhard Heinrich	Weimar	
AMME, Johann Andreas Gottlieb	Allstedt	
AMME, Johanna Ernestine, born Stieber	Allstedt	
ANGELROTH, Johan Michel	Ollendorf	with wife and 3 children
APEL, Auguste	Weimar	
BAERMANN, Adolf Eduard	Niedergrunstedt	with wife Ida Wilhelmine and 1 child
BAMBERG, Wilhelm August	Albendorf	saddler and harness maker; with wife Karoline
BARTMANN, Christian Friedrich	Hottelstedt	
BARTMANN, Katharina Regina	Hottelstedt	with 2 children
BAUCHSPIESS, Friedrich Wilhelm Martin	Klettbach	with 1 child
BAUMANN, Auguste Wilhelmine Marie	Weimar	
BAUMEISTER, --	Rastenberg	Surgeon; with wife Charlotte, born Schroeter, and 4 children

Emigrant's Name	Place of Origin	Remarks
BECK, Christoph Bernhard	Hopfgarten	
BECKER, Eduard	Ulla	
BEINZE, Johann Christian	Weimar	gardener; with wife Susanne Marie, born Büttcher, and 3 children
BERGMEYER, Ernestine	Taubach	
BERLT, Carl ERnst Christian	Berlstedt	hand laborer
BERNECKER, Gotthold	Hadisleben	journeyman baker
BESTEL, Christoph Friedrich	Allstedt	master sackmaker [*Beutlermeister*]
BESTEL, Marie Sophie Dorothea, born Goldschmidt	Allstedt	
BLAU, Friedrich Bernhard Ludwig	Rietnord-hausen	
BLAU, Johann Heinrich Friedrich	Rietnord-hausen	
BLOSS, Karoline Marianne	Berlstädt	
BLUMENSTEIN, Johanne Henriette Bernhardine	Bucha	
BOEHMITZ, Karl Friedrich	Oldisleben	journeyman shoemaker
BOERNER, Christian Samuel	Apolda	master knitter [*Wirkermeister*, underwear, stockings, etc.]; with wife

Emigrant's Name	Place of Origin	Remarks
BOERNER, Friedrich Wilhelm	Oldisleben	Hand laborer
BORN, Johann Ernst	Wipfra	
BORNSCHEIN, Friedrich Wilhelm	Nirmsdorf	
BOTHMANN, Heinrich	Oldisleben	master shoemaker; with wife and 2 children
BRAEUTIGAM, Johann Ernst Theodor	Rettwitz	
BRAEUTIGAM, Nikolaus Theodor Heinrich	Nieder- zimmern	
BRANDT, Heinrich Emil Theodor	Eckstädt	
BRANDT, Johann Theodor Wilhelm	Eckstädt	
BREHM, Auguste	Martinroda	
BROEMMER, Johann Theo- dor	Vieselbach	
BRUECKNER, Auguste	Kiliansroda	
BRUECKNER, Heinrich	Kiliansroda	
BRUECKNER, Jakob	Kiliansroda	with wife and 2 children
BRUECKNER, Johanna Henriette, born Rose	Remda	
BRUECKNER, Heinrich	Kiliansroda	
BRUECKNER, Maria Elisa- betha	Kiliansroda	
BUCHMANN, Rosalie	Mittelhausen	daughter of a farmer [*Landw.*

Emigrant's Name	Place of Origin	Remarks
BUCHSPIES, Christiane Friederike Auguste	Troistedt	
BUCHSPIES, Johann Carl	Troistedt	
BUCHSPIES, Johann Carl Friedrich	Troistedt	hand laborer
BUCHSPIES, Martha Elisabeth, born Kästner	Troistedt	
BUCHSPIES, Wilhelm	Troistedt	
BUETTNER, Friederike	--	with 1 child
BURCKHARDT, Gottlieb	Zottelstedt	
BURKHARDT, Christian Heinrich	Kleinlohma	
BURKHARDT, Heinrich	Maina	master weaver; with wife and 1 child
BURKHARDT, Johann Friedrich	Wöllnitz	
BURKHARDT, Rosina, born Graf	Maina	
CHRIST, Johann Heinrich August	Mellingen	
CLAUS, Karl Friedrich	Wetzdorf	
CONRAD, Adeline	Neustadt	
DAENSTEDT, Johann Heinrich	Leutenthal	
DECKERT, Friedrich Samuel	Winkel	master tailor; with wife and 4 children

Emigrant's Name	Place of Origin	Remarks
DEGLIMES, Paul Franz	Mundkoch, Weimar	with wife Sophie, 7 children and 1 granddaughter [see Ludwig]
DEINHARDT, Johann Martin Daniel	Hopfgarten	
DENSTEDT, Marie	Hopfgarten	
DERAME [Deramé] Karl Friedrich August	Taubach	with wife Charlotte Karoline
DITTMAR, Johann Christian	Grossrudestedt	
DIEZ, Gotthold Friedrich	Ettersburg	
DONAT, Wilhelmine	Rastenberg	
DRESSLER, Johann Nikolaus	Heyda	
EBELING, Friedrich Wilhelm	Wolferstedt	journeyman baker
ECKARDT, Johann Georg Theodor	Jena	unloader; with wife and 3 children
ECKARDT, Karl Julius	Uppferstedt	
EHRHARDT, Friedrich	Vogelsberg	with wife Marie and 1 child
EHRLICH, Karl Friedrich August	Naschhausen	
EILENSTEIN, Adam	Hainichen	with wife Dorothea Elisabeth, born Scheide
EILENSTEIN, Johann Friedrich Traugott	Hainichen	with wife Karoline, born Röder
EILHAUER, Johann Georg Friedrich	Stadtremda	with wife and 2 children

Emigrant's Name	Place of Origin	Remarks
ELLE, Johann Georg	Martinroda	
ENGEL, Johann Philipp	Schwerstedt	with 1 child
ENGLER, Julius Robert	Weimar	businessman [*Handlungskommis*]
ESPE, Heinrich	Buttelstedt	hand laborer
EWALD, Johann Christoph	Olbersleben	
FEISTKORN, Johann Heinrich Theodor	Ollendorf	
FICKERT, Karl Friedrich August	Weimar	
FISCHER, Therese	Kleinlöbichau	
FOERSTER, Friedrich August	Rannstedt	
FRANKE, Henriette Karoline	Weimar	
FRANZ, Juliane Wilhelmine	Weimar	
FRATSCHER, August	Neuengörs?	
FREIBERG, Johann Ernst	Dienstedt	
FRITSCH, Friedrich August	Hochstädt	with wife and 3 children
FRITSCH, Heinrich	Berlstedt	
FROEHLICH, Gottlieb	Liebsdorf	
FROEHLICH, Gottfried	Liebsdorf	
FUCHS, Johann Ernst	Grossrudestedt	with wife and 1 child

Emigrant's Name	Place of Origin	Remarks
GADERMANN, Johann Christian Heinrich	Radersdorf	with 3 children
GEBHARDT, Maria Christiane Henriette	Legefe?	
GEHRING, Robert Edmund Hugo	Blankenhain	
GEISS, Johann Christoph	Rettwitz	
GEIST, Johann Wilhelm	Berka am Ilm	master shoemaker
GELMROTH, Friedrich	Stadtremda	with 4 children
GENGELBACH, Karl August	Buttstädt	
GERBER, Carl August Moritz	Ottmannshausen	wagon and wheelwright [Stellmacher] journeyman
GERDEN, Christiane Franziska	Weimar	with child
GERLACH, August	Kospeda	
GERLACH, Friedrich	Kospeda	
GERSTENBERG, Johann Georg	Kleinschwabhausen	with wife Marie Sophie, born Giltsch, and 6 children
GEYER, Friederike Luise	Buttelstedt	
GEYER, Heinrich Theodor	Grossrudestedt	
GEYER, Johanna Dorothea	Kirchremda	with children
GIESSLER, Christian Eduard	Schlossvippach	
GIESSLER, Marie Sophie	Schlossvippach	

Emigrant's Name	Place of Origin	Remarks
GNICHTEL, Luise	Blankenhain	with 1 child
GOEPFARDT, Johann Heinrich Wilhelm	Niedersynderstedt	
GOETZE, Nikolaus Wilhelm Friedrich Hermann	Jena	business assistant
GOTTSCHALG, Bernhard	Taubach	master linen weaver; with wife
GOTTSCHALG, Friedrich Wilhelm Ferdinand	Taubach	
GOTTSCHALG [or Gottschlag], Johann Christoph	Kiliansroda	with wife
GOTTSCHLAG, Friederike, born Brückner		
GRAEFE, Georg Friedrich	Kunitz	with wife
GRAEFE, Johanne Christiane, born Knabe	--	with children
GRASSAU, Adelgunde Wilhelmine	Vollersroda	
GRAU, Friederike, born Winne	Kleinschwabhausen	
GRAU, Johann Heinrich	Kleinschwabhausen	with wife
GRAU, Rosina, born Marquardt		with 3 children
GRENZEL, Johann Philipp	Buttelstedt	
GROLL, Friedrich Eduard	Zottelstedt	
GROSSE, Eva Friederike	Ulrichshalben	

Emigrant's Name	Place of Origin	Remarks
GROSSE, Heinrich Samuel	Ulrichshalben	with wife
GROSSE, Anna Christine	--	with 2 children
GROSSKOPF, Friederike Christiane	Albendorf	
GUENSCHMANN, Friedrich	Neusiss	
GUENSCHMANN, Johanna	Neusiss	
GUENSCHMANN, Therese	Neusiss	
GUENTHER, Gottlob	Grossbrembach	with wife and 1 child
HAAGEN, Wilhelm Karl	Oldisleben	journeyman furniture maker
HAENSGEN, Christian Friedrich August	Taubach	
HALLE, Heinrich	Grossbrembach	with wife and 4 children
HALLE, Johann Wilhelm	Schwerstedt	
HANEMANN, Wilhelm August Albert	Dornburg	
HARTMANN, Adam Heinrich Friedrich	Güttern	with wife and 3 children
HARTUNG, Dorothea Luise	Stadtremda	with 1 illegitimate child
HARTUNG, Josephine Esther Linna	Weimar	
HASE, Karl Christoph Martin	Hopfgarten	
HEBESTREIT, Maria Barbara	Tottleben	

Emigrant's Name	Place of Origin	Remarks
HEIM, Johann Christian Friedrich	Stadtremda	master shoemaker
HEIMBOLD, Heinrich	Cospeda	with 5 children
HEINE, Johann Georg Ferdinand	Berlstädt	with wife and 6 children
HEINEL, Friedrich Emil	Legefeld	
HEINEMANN, Johanna Marie Friederike	Troistedt	
HEINICKE, Emilie Charlotte	Apolda	
HEINTZE, Johanne Christiane	Remda	
HELBING, Beate Auguste Pauline	Berka am Ilm	
HELFER, Johann Ernst	Sohstädt	with wife and 3 children
HELM, Carl Friedrich Gustav	Weida	journeyman weaver
HEMME, Gottgold	Grossbrembach	journeyman carpenter; with wife and 1 child
HEUNE, Karl Friedrich Andreas	Olbersleben	
HEUNSCH, Gustav Adolf Bernhard	Stadtremda	
HEUSCHKEL, Marta Susanna	Kranichborn	
HEUSCHKEL, Wilhelm Bernhard	Kranichborn	
HEYMUELLER, Johann Philipp	Magdala	with wife

Emigrant's Name	Place of Origin	Remarks
HEYMUELLER, Dorothea, born Kuerschner	--	
HILDEBRAND, Johann Heinrich, Senior	Buttstädt	
HILDEBRAND, Johann Heinrich, Junior	--	with wife and 3 children
HILDEBRANDT, Heinrich	Possendorf	
HOFMANN, Johann Ernst	Mittelhausen	master mason
HOFMANN, Johanna Marie Margarethe, born Fischer	Mittelhausen	
HOFMANN, Wilhelmine	Mittelhausen	
HOLLBACH, Johann Michael	Sundremda	hand laborer; with wife, 9 children, and 1 illegitimate grandson
HOYER, Henriette Karoline	Stotternheim	
HUEHNE, Johanna Marie	Buttelstedt	
HUELLE, Georg Bernhard	Mittelhausen	
HUELLE, Therese Wilhelmine	Mittelhausen	
INSINGER, Johann Friedrich Emil	Weimar	
INSNER, Johann[e?], born Schenk	Buttstädt	
INSNER, Moritz	Buttstädt	with wife and 2 children

Emigrant's Name	Place of Origin	Remarks
JACOBI, Franz August	Büsleben	
JACOBI, Heinrich Friedrich Eduard	Gelmeroda	with wife, 2 children, and 2 stepsons Körner
JACOBI, Johann Andreas	Gelmeroda	with wife and 3 children
JAHN, Joseph Eustachius	Berka am Ilm	with wife and 3 children
KAEFERHAUS, Hermann	Allstedt	
KAEFERHAUS, Marie Christiane, born Gothe	Allstedt	
KAEFERHAUS, Wilhelm Ferdinand	Allstedt	hand laborer
KAESTNER, Rosine Wilhelmine Auguste	Rietnordhausen	
KAHLE, Johann Andreas Gottlob	Hanichen	with wife and 2 children
KAISER, Johann Andreas	Utzberg	with wife and 6 children
KARPE, Georg Andreas	Grossbrembach	with wife and 2 children
KARPE, Friedrich Wilhelm	Grossbrembach	with wife and 3 children
KAUFMANN, Johann Gottfried	Tümmelsdorf	farmer [Landwirt]
KEIMLING, Gottlob Bernard	Reisdorf	
KEIMLING, Ferdinand Julius	Reisdorf	
KIRCHNER, Anna	Troistedt	
KIRCHNER, FRIEDERIKE	Troistedt	

Emigrant's Name	*Place of Origin*	*Remarks*
KIRCHNER, Friedrich Franz	Troistedt	
KIRCHNER, Marie Dorothea	Troistedt	
KIRSCH, Johanna Christiane Judith	Maina	
KITTELMANN, Wilhelmine Ernestine	Neustadt	
KLEINE, Wilhelm Alexander	Apolda	
KNABE, Friedrich Anton	Schwarza	with wife and 5 children
KNABE, Johann Georg Ferdinand	Schwarza	with wife and 2 children
KNOCHE, Johann Heinrich Gottlieb	Heygendorf	
KOCH, Christoph Elias	Martinroda	
KOCH, Friedrich Eduard	Buttelstedt	
KOCH, Henriette Wilhelmine, born Schauerhammer	Lobeda	with 3 children
KOCH, Karl August	Wormstedt	with wife
KOCH, Rosine Friederike, born Henschel	--	with 1 child
KOCH, Marie Rosine, born Tischler	Oberndorf	with 5 children
KOEHLER, Dorothea Sophia	Kranichborn	with 1 child
KOEHLER, Ernst Emil	Taupadel	
KOENIG, Johann Friedrich Heinrich	Magdala	

Emigrant's Name	Place of Origin	Remarks
KOERNER, Christian Theodor	Gelmeroda	hand laborer
KOETSCHAU, Johann Andreas	Umpferstedt	with wife and 2 children
KOHLMANN, Herrmann	Olbersleben	servant [Knecht]
KOPPE, Christian	Kunitz	
KRAUSPE, Karl Konstantin	Wogau	
KRAUSSE, Johann Friedrich	Azmannsdorft	with wife
KRAUSSE, Marie Dorothea, born Machts	--	with 6 children
KREBS, Friedrich	Kleinobringen	with wife and 2 children
KRELLWITZ, Wilhelm	Olbersleben	
KREUBEL, Johann Friedrich	Sundremda	
KREUZBERG, Johann Karl	Krautheim	master shoemaker; with 2 children
KRIEGER, Johann Heinrich Georg	Weimar	journeyman potter
KRUMBHOLZ, Karl Friedrich	Cottendorf	
KRUPPE, Johann Heinrich August	Rietnordhausen	
KUEHN, Friedrich Wilhelm Emil	Kranichfeld	
KUEHN, Gustav Edmund Rudolph	Kleinromstedt	
KUERSTEN, Karl Friedrich	Sundremda	

Emigrant's Name	Place of Origin	Remarks
KUNZE, Christian	Poppendorf	journeyman carpenter; with
KUNZE, Eleonore, born Blütner	--	
LANGBEIN, Christine	Hopfgarten	with 2 children
LANGBEIN, Johann Karl	Kleinkromsdorf	
LANGENBERG, Friedrich August Hermann	Ramsla	
LANGENBERG, Friederike	Berka am Ilm	with 1 child
LEILACH, Ida, born Burkhardt	Auma	
LEITLOFF, Johann Christoph Adolf	Tonndorf	
LEITLOFF, Johann Friedrich Richard	Tonndorf	
LEITLOFF, Johann Wilhelm	Tonndorf	
LEITSOH, Ernst	Rietnordhausen	coachman
LEONHARD, Paul	Krautheim	journeyman furniture maker
LERCHE, Rosalie Clara	Oldisleben	
LERZ, August	Schwarza	
LERZ, Bertha	Schwarza	
LERZ, Heinrich	Schwarza	
LEY, Ernst Albert	Blankenhain	
LIEBESKIND, Barbara	Güttern	

Emigrant's Name	Place of Origin	Remarks
LIEBESKIND, Dorothea Elisabeth	Güttern	
LIEBESKIND, Eva Maria	Güttern	with 2 children
LIEBESKIND, Johanna Christiane	--	
LOCH, Johann Andreas Wilhelm	Lehnstedt	with wife and 1 child
LOCKE, Johann Christoph	Güttern	with wife and 2 children
LOEBNITZ, Christoph Friedrich	Zottelstedt	
LOESER, Johann Friedrich Georg	Hassleben	with wife and 3 children
LORBER, August	Rastenberg	hand laborer
LORENZ, Johann Georg Anton	Weimar	
LOTHOLZ, Karl August Reinhold	Buttstädt	
LUDWIG, Josephine, born Deglimes	--	with 3 children [see Deglimes herein]
MAEDEL, Justina Friederike, born Pape	Weimar	with 5 children
MALECH, Carl Wilhelm August	Liebstädt	master tailor
MANN, Bernhard Adolf Hugo	Dornburg	
MARKGRAF, Johann Wilhelm	Hassleben	

Emigrant's Name	Place of Origin	Remarks
MARQUART, Johanna Marie Therese	Kleinschwab- hausen	
METZ, Frieda Gerike Sophie, born Dom- rich	Oldisleben	
MISSLITZ, Karl Wilhelm August	Küssnitz	with wife
MISSLITZ, Karoline, born Stahl	--	with 4 children
MITWEIDE, Christian Gottfried Zacharias	Damm- häusern	with wife
MITWEIDE, Ernestine, born Triefelmann	--	with 4 children
MOELLER, Christiane	Sohnstedt	
MOELLER, Caroline	Sohnstedt	
MOELLER, Gottlieb Michael	Stotternheim	
MOELLER, Johann Friedrich	Sohnstedt	
MOELLER, Johanna Christiane Luise	Stadtremda	
MOEHRING, Elisabeth Friederike	Heilsberg	
MOENCHGESANG, Johann Gottlieb	Hassleben	master shoemaker; with wife and 1 child
MUELLER, Constantin	Gebstedt	
MUELLER, Johann Andreas	Albendorf	with wife
MUELLER, Christiane Karoline, born Wohl- rabe	--	with 4 children

Emigrant's Name	Place of Origin	Remarks
MUELLER, Johann August Ferdinand	Weiden	
MUELLER, Karl Wilhelm	Weimar	
MUELBERG, Nikolaus	Sohnstedt	with wife and 1 child
MUENZEL, Louis	Buttelstedt	
<u>NAGEL</u>, Johann Carl Christian	Allstedt	
<u>NAGEL</u>, Johanne Friederike, born Lungershausen	Allstedt	
NICOLAI, Johann Georg	Niederzimmern	with wife
NICOLAI, Anna Maria Luise	--	with 1 child
NOCH, Johann Friedrich Moritz	Jena	master shoemaker; with wife
NOELLER, Johanne Christiane Luise	Stadtremda	
NOELLERT, Johann Friedrich	Winzerla	
NOTH, Heinrich Friedrich	Nauendorf	with wife
NOTH, Marta Sibille	--	with 4 children
NUERNBERGER, Johann Gottlob	Vieselbach	master tailor; with wife and 3 children
NUERNBERGER, Johann Traugott	Vieselbach	master tailor; with wife and 2 children

Emigrant's Name	Place of Origin	Remarks
OBERREICH, Georg Christoph	Grossbrembach	
OTTO, Friedrich Ernst Theodor	Allstedt	presently lessee of a tavern [*Pachtschenkenwirt*] in Mittelhausen; with wife
OTTO, Ludowine, born Reinecke	--	with 1 child
PABST, Johann Andreas	Oldisleben	hand laborer
PABST, Johanna, born Hofmann	Oldisleben	[*see also* Hofmann]
PAPPE, Nikolaus Theodor	Hopfgarten	
PETTERS, Heinrich Karl	Blankenhain	
PFEIFFER, Ernestine, born Fröhlich	Weida	[*see also* Froehlich]
POERTZEL, Karl Friedrich Wilhlem	Blankenhain	master glazier
POLLAND, Friedrich	Essleben	with wife and 3 children
POLLAND, Friedrich Christian	Essleben	
POSER, Christian Friedrich Theodor	Kranichfeld	with wife
POSER, Franziska, born Becher	--	
PREISSER, Ida Elisabeth	Kleinbrembach	with illegitimate child
PREISSER, Johann Karl Christoph	Roedigen	with his wife

Emigrant's Name	Place of Origin	Remarks
PREISSER, Hanne Rosette, born Röthling	--	with 1 child
PRELLER, Friedrich Sebald	Süssenborn	
PUTSCHE, Dorothea	Umpferstedt	with 5 children
RAEUBER, Johann Heinrich Christoph	Kleinobritzgen?	
RANKE, Charlotte Wilhelmine Karoline	Apolda	
REICH, Johann Ernst	Hochdorf	
REICHARDT, Theodor	Weiden	with wife
REICHARDT, Friederike	--	with 2 children
REIFSCHNEIDER, Johann Andreas Bernhard	Marvippach?	with wife
REIM, Eva Maria Therese, born Münch	Germannshausen?	with 2 children
REISE, Johann Peter	Ollendorf	
ROESSING, Karl Friedrich Julius	Rannstedt	
ROETSCH, Karl Eduard Gottlieb	Weimar	master tailor; with wife and 7 children
ROSE, Georg Christoph Julius	Kleinpürschütz	
ROSENBERGER, Günter Karl Anton	Tonndorf	
ROST, Johann Heinrich	Trübsdorf	

Emigrant's Name	Place of Origin	Remarks
ROST, Johann Sebald	Udestedt	
ROTTSTEDT, Johann Georg	Stotternheim	with wife and 3 children
ROTTMANN, Ernst	Martinroda	with wife and 3 children
ROTTMANN, Heinrich Christoph	Martinroda	with wife
SAUERBREI, Bernhard	Martinroda	with wife
SAUERBREI, Marie, born Koch	--	with 3 children
SAUL, Johann Nikolaus	Hopfgarten	with 4 children and 5 step-children
SAUL, Margarete	Ottstedt	with 4 children
SCHAEFER, Johann Christoph Heinrich	Winkel	barber's helper
SCHAEFER, Johann Heinrich	Bösleben	with wife
SCHAEFER, Marie Sophie	--	
SCHEER, Johann Heinrich Friedrich Conrad	Buttstädt	Master broom and brush maker; with wife
SCHEER, Wilhelmine, born Müller	--	with 3 children
SCHEIBE, Gottfried	Laasan	with wife
SCHEIBE, Maria Elisabeth, born Müller	--	with 7 children
SCHELLENSCHLAEGER, Johann Christoph	Troistedt	hand worker

Emigrant's Name	Place of Origin	Remarks
SCHLEEVOGT, Hermann Christian Gotthold	Buttelstedt	
SCHLEVOIGT, Karl Bern- hard Gotthilf	Rohrbach	
SCHLUND, Johann Georg	Neusitz	with stepdaughter
SCHMEDCHEN, Johann Friedrich Immanuel	Buttstädt	master shoemaker; with wife and 2? children
SCHMID, David	Kiliansroda	mayor
SCHMIDT, August	Zwätzen	with wife
SCHMIDT, Pauline, born Eilenstein	--	with 1 child
SCHMIDT, Christian	Zwätzen	with wife
SCHMIDT, Elisabeth, born Hage	--	
SCHMIDT, Friedrich August	Jena	master weaver; with wife
SCHMIDT, Auguste Mag- dalene, born Müller	--	with 1 child
SCHMIDT, Georg Hein- rich Theodor	Utzberg	master blacksmith; with wife
SCHMIDT, Gustav Eduard	Auma	cloth maker [Tuchmacher]
SCHMIDT, Johann Friedrich	Ballstedt	with wife and 2 children
SCHMIDT, Johann Mi- chael Eduard	Vieselbach	with wife and 2 children
SCHMIDT, Johanna Doro- thea Wilhelmine	Utzberg	

Emigrant's Name	Place of Origin	Remarks
SCHMIDT, Marta Benigna	Niederzimmern	with 3 children
SCHMIDT, Wilhelm Heinrich	Büsleben	with wife and 2 children
SCHNEIDER, Karoline	Magdala	
SCHOENEMANN, Johann Friedrich	Udestedt	with 1 child
SCHOENEMANN, Wilhelm David	Mittelhausen	farmer [*Landwirt*]
SCHORCHT, Johann Friedrich Wilhelm	Jena	hand worker
SCHRAMM, Christian Friedrich	Martinroda	
SCHREYER, Gottlob Huldreich	Wolferstedt	with wife
SCHREYER, Marie Magdalene, born Ermisch	--	
SCHREYER, Karl Gottlob	Wolferstedt	
SCHROEDER, Johann Heinrich Christoph	Kiliansroda	
SCHROEPFER, Friedrich Christian Theodor	Vieselbach	
SCHUCHARDT, Julius Konstantin	Obdrreissen	restaurateuer [*Oeconom*]; with wife and 2 children
SCHUEFFLER, Heinrich Theodor	Troistedt	
SCHUMANN, Magdalene	Dielsdorf	unmarried, with 7-year-old child
SCHWEINFURT, Gottlieb	Ilmenau	glazier; with wife and 2 children

Emigrant's Name	Place of Origin	Remarks
SCHWEITZER, Richard	Neustadt	adept at restaurant work [*Oeconomiebeflissener*]
SENFTLEBEN, Friederike	Buttelstedt	
SENFTLEBEN, Johann Karl Adolf	Buttelstedt	master furniture maker; with wife
SENFTLEBEN, Johanna, born Gebhardt	--	
SIEBER, Andreas Otto	Kleinlöbichau	
SIEBOLD, Christian Friedrich Karl	Mellingen	
SIMMROTH, Dorothea, born Möbius	Allstedt	
SIMMROTH, Johann Andreas Gottfried	Allstedt	
SOELGMAR, Elise, born Waldmann	Niedergrun-stedt	
SOELGMAR, Friedrich Louis	Niedergrun-stedt	with wife
SOELGMAR, Emma	--	with 3 children
SONNEKALB, Friedrich August Gottlob	Lobeda	
SONNEKALB, Carl Fried-rich Christian	Lobeda	
SONNENSCHEIN, Frieder-ike Dorothea Karo-line, born Schwarz	Lobeda	
SPREER, Johann Moritz Eduard	Weimar	master shoemaker

Emigrant's Name	Place of Origin	Remarks
SPRENGLER, Friedrich Gottlieb	Allstedt	master butcher; with wife
SPRENGLER, Johanna Charlotte, born Brauer	--	
STEINBRUECK, Andreas	Ballstedt	with wife and 1 child
STEINACKER, Dorothea Charlotte Wilhelmine	--	with 3 illegitimate children
STEINBOCK, Carl Friedrich	Markersdorf	master weaver; with family
STIEBRITZ, Johanna	Jena	with 1 child
STOECKEL, Friedrich	Frauenpreissnitz	hand worker
STOECKEL, Leonhard August Hermann	Buchfart	
STRASBURG, Marie	Grossschwabhausen	
STROMEYER, Franz	Weimar	court musician; with wife and 4 children
TAUBERT, Friedrich	Stadtbürgel	journeyman carpenter
TECHAND, Wilhelmine	Wenigenjena	with 1 child
TEUCHERT, Maria	Kiliansroda	
THALDORF, Susanne	Kranichfeld	
THYROLF, Gottfried Hermann Leberecht	Hirschroda	
TISCHER, Friedrich August	Vieselbach	with wife and 2 children

Emigrant's Name	Place of Origin	Remarks
TISCHER, Georg Adam	Schwerstedt	
TISCHER, Amalie	Schwerstedt	
TISCHER, Karl Friedrich	Schwerstedt	
TISCHER, Marie Elisabeth	Schwerstedt	
TISCHNER, Friedrich Hermann	Schwerstedt	[so spelled]
TOEPFER, Friedrich	Stadtremda	master butcher; with wife and 5 children
TOPF, Heinrich Louis	Ottstedt	with wife and 1 child
TOPF, Karl Moritz Heinrich	Kranichfeld	
TRAENKLER, Christine, born Schroeder	Allstedt	
TRAENKLER, August Wilhelm Michael	Allstedt	
TROESTER, Elise Therese	Oldisleben	
VOGEL, Johann Gottfried	Kunitz	with wife and 3 children
VOLLAND, Johann Leopold	Gutmannshausen	with wife and 8 children
WAECHTER, Johann Christian August	Stadtremda	master furniture maker; with wife and 1 child
WAELDCHEN, Johann Christoph	Schlossvippach	
WAGNER, Karl Eduard	Sohnstedt	

Emigrant's Name	Place of Origin	Remarks
WAGNER, Johann Gottfried	Allstedt	master tailor; with wife
WAGNER, Amalie Catharina, born Deutsch	--	
WALLBURG, Johann Georg	Essleben	with wife
WALLBURG, Dorothea, born Laue	--	with 1 child
WALLBURG, Marie, born Weckesser	Essleben	
WALTER, Andreas	Zwätzen	with wife
WALTER, Johanna, born Ritter	--	with 6 children
WALTHER, Johann Bernhard	Hassleben	with wife
WALTHER, Johanna Magdalene Karoline	Ollendorf	
WALTHER, Marie	Wolferstedt	
WASSMANN, Karl Friedrich Wilhelm	Allstedt	journeyman tailor
WEHLING, Georg	Dornburg	
WEINHOLD, Friedrich	Sundremda	hand worker; with wife and 4 children
WEINHOLD, Johann Christoph	Sundremda	
WEINHOLD, Rosine Christiane, born Medius	Sundremda	
WEINLAND, Anton Louis	Vippachedelhausen	with wife

Emigrant's Name	Place of Origin	Remarks
WEINLAND, Karoline Friederike	--	
WEISE, Auguste Luise	Ulla	
WEISSLEDER, Christian Friedrich August	Jena	master blacksmith; with wife Luise, born Boehme, and 2 children
WENDELMUTH, Dorothea Elisabeth	Neckerode	with 1 child
WENZEL, Karl Friedrich August	Umpferstedt	with wife and 1 child
WERNER, Johann Friedrich Ludwig	Schoppendorf	
WERNER, Johann Heinrich August Theodor	Tiefengruben	with wife and 2 children
WIEGAND, Karoline Laura	Blankenhain	
WIESENBURG, Heinrich	Hopfgarten	with wife and 1 child
WIMMLER, Georg Theodor Anton	Ilmenau	
WINNE, Valentin Wilhelm	Grosskromsdorf	with 2 children
WIPPRECHT, Johann Christoph Wilhelm	Stotternheim	with wife and 3 children
WOLF, Johann Wilhelm	Weimar	gardener; with wife and 4 children
ZEH, Auguste Therese	Gutmannshausen	

Emigrant's Name	Place of Origin	Remarks
ZIEHN, Johann August	Rietnord-hausen	with wife and 2 children
ZINK, Heinrich Theo-dor	Weimar	
ZOELLNER, Anna Fried-erike Amalie	Kunitz	
ZOELLNER, Johanna Luise	Kunitz	
ZSCHIEGNER, Johann Friedrich Ferdi-nand	Dörtendorf	master weaver; with wife and 2 children